Cape York, Cooktown Travel Guide, North Queensland Australia

Great Barrier Reef Environment Touristic Guide

Author
David Mills.

SONITTEC PUBLISHING. All rights reserved. No part of this publication may be reproduced, distributed, or transmitted in any form or by any means, including photocopying, recording, or other electronic or mechanical methods, without the prior written permission of the publisher, except in the case of brief quotations embodied in critical reviews and certain other noncommercial uses permitted by copyright law. For permission requests, write to the publisher, addressed "Attention: Permissions Coordinator," at the address below.

Copyright © 2019 Sonittec Publishing
All Rights Reserved

First Printed: 2019.

Publisher:
SONITTEC LTD
College House, 2nd Floor
17 King Edwards Road,
Ruislip
London
HA4 7AE

Table of Content

SUMMARY 1
CAPE YORK INTRODUCTION 4
COOKTOWN 6
Attractions 10
- James Cook Museum (National Trust of Queensland) 14
- Nature's Powerhouse 15
- Cooktown Creative Arts Association 16
- Cooktown Bowls Club 17

Things to See and Do 17
Places of interest 50
- The Boathouse, Cooktown Re-enactment Association 50
- Lions Den Hotel 52
- Walker Bay and Quarantine Bay 54
- Archer Point 54
- Cooktown History Centre 55

Places to Eat 56
- Lions Den Hotel 56
- Balcony Restaurant 58
- Annan's Restaurant 58
- Restaurant 1770 59

Accommodation 60
- Cooktown Harbour Views Luxury Apartments 60
- Cooktown Alamanda Inn 61
- Milkwood Lodge 62
- Sovereign Resort Hotel 63
- Cooktown Holiday Park 64
- Cooktown Caravan Park 65

Fast Guide 65
Tour 74
- Hidden Valley Trail Rides 74
- Cooktown Barrier Reef Fishing Charters 75
- Cooktown Barra Charters 76
- Cooktown Adventure Camping and Scenic Tours 77
- Bloomfield River Water Sports 77
- Bungie Helicopters 78

- Cooktown Glass Bottom Boat and Dinghy Hire 79
- Gone Fishing..79
- Daintree Air Services...80
- Yuku Baja Muliku..81
- Great Northern Tours 84

LOWER CAPE 85

Attractions 85
- Chillagoe-Mungana Caves National Park..........................85
- Quinkan & Regional Cultural Centre.................................86
- Hopevale Arts & Cultural Centre 88
- Bana Yirriji Art & Cultural Centre......................................90

Accommodation 91
- Lizard Island 91
- Laura Motel..91
- Lotusbird Lodge..92
- Bloomfield Beach House 94
- Bloomfield Lodge..95
- Bloomfield Beach Camp...96
- Hann River Roadhouse..99
- Cape Tribulation Camping..99
- Palmer River Roadhouse..100
- Mount Carbine Caravan Park 101

Places of Interest.. 103
- Daintree...103
- Pormpuraaw 104
- Laura 106
- Kowanyama 108
- Hopevale...110

CENTRAL CAPE 113

Places of Interest.. 115
- Wunthulpu Visitor Centre, Coen 115
- Coen Heritage House...116

Summary

The world is a book and those who do not travel read only one page.

It is indeed very unfortunate that some people feel traveling is a sheer waste of time, energy and money. Some also find traveling an extremely boring activity. Nevertheless, a good majority of people across the world prefer traveling, rather than staying inside the confined spaces of their homes. They love to explore new places, meet new people, and see things that they would not find in their homelands. It is this very popular attitude that has made tourism, one of the most profitable, commercial sectors in the world.

People travel for various reasons. Some travel for work, others for fun, and some for finding mental peace. Though every person may have his/her own reason to go on a journey, it is essential to note that traveling, in itself, has some inherent advantages. For one, for some days getting away from everyday routine is a pleasant change. It not only refreshes one's body, but also mind and soul. Traveling to a distant place and doing exciting things that are not thought of otherwise, can rejuvenate a person, who then returns home, ready to take on new and more difficult challenges in life and work. It makes a person forget his worries, problems, frustrations, and fears, albeit for some time. It gives him a chance to think wisely and constructively. Traveling also helps to heal; it can mend a broken heart.

For many people, traveling is a way to attain knowledge, and perhaps, a quest to find answers to their questions. For this, many people prefer to go to faraway and isolated places. For believers, it is a search for God and to gain higher knowledge; for others, it is a search for inner peace. They might or might not find what they are looking for, but such an experience certainly enriches their lives

Cape York Introduction

Cape York is on many people's 'Bucket List' for good reason. Under the following loactions are covered for the best touristic travel experience. COOKTOWN, WESTERN CAPE, NPA & TORRES STRAIT, CENTRAL CAPE, IRON RANGE, LOWER CAPE. SURE, it has the northern most piece of land on the Australian continent, but don't rush to get there! The Peninsula is a vast and diverse landscape offering a myriad of adventures and side trips off the beaten path. Take a detour through Rinyirru National Park (Lakefield) and see the abundant birdlife surrounding lagoons and wetlands; better yet, throw a line in and try your luck catching the famous barramundi Cape York is renowned for.

Cape York also has many pristine beaches that can be easily accessed, and nesting turtles can be seen at the right time of the year. Excellent bush camping, inside and outside of the National Parks, can be enjoyed throughout the region, and facilities are available at certain destinations- see the National Parks Section; all camping in National Parks must now be booked in advance.

For the fishing enthusiast, there are also plenty of options, whether it's fishing off the local wharf, along one of the Cape's majestic rivers, or taking advantage of the local knowledge of the many charter tour operators. Have a look at the fishing section and experience some world class fishing today. Enjoy your trip!

Cooktown

Nestled between the mouth of the Endeavour River and Grassy Hill, with Mt Cook as a backdrop, Cooktown is a charming, historical town, unspoilt by the urgency of modern life. Its close proximity to the Endeavour and Annan Rivers, and nearby reefs, make it an ideal fishing destination. Cooktown is a good base for those wanting to do day trips north to Elim Beach, across to Laura, or south to Bloomfield, but it is too out of the way to reach many of the other attractions of the lower Cape (people with caravans can leave them here or in Laura, to continue on to Cape York). Cooktown is known for is its well documented history, including the first known European contact with the Indigenous people of this region, after Captain Cook ran aground on some reefs off the coast. Later it became a bustling port, exporting gold from the Palmer River Goldfields, and had 47 licensed pubs within the town boundaries in 1874; today there are still a few along the main street to stop and grab a cold one.

So, step back in time and enjoy some of the heritage buildings, monuments, and centres around town paying homage to an era of great hardship and triumph. Cooktown has a visitor information centre within the Nature's Powerhouse complex, at the end of Walker Street. This is a good place to start exploring Cooktown. Nature's Powerhouse is within the historic Botanic Gardens, and features the Vera Scarth-Johnson Gallery, the Charles Tanner Wildlife of Cape York Queensland Museum Exhibition, a Book and Gift Shop, and Vera's Café. While you're there, pick up a copy of "Explore Cooktown", a small guide produced by the local chamber of commerce to provide more detail on the local history and attractions.

Holidays & Vacations - Travel & Tourism

Cooktown is not only the perfect setting for a holiday in total luxury with tropical surroundings but it is also a town full of history and artefacts dating back to the years of Captain James Cook. Be prepared to experience a holiday like no other as you step back in time, as you immerse yourself in the town's history as well as the million year old rainforest that surrounds you.

Within Cooktown you will be treated to exquisite dining, luxury accommodation, activities to great to name, attractions galore and excellent shopping which we all love to do while you are on holidays. As you wander the streets of the northern town in Queensland you find it hard not to completely immerse yourself in the vibrant atmosphere that is part of this tropical town. There beautiful parks and gardens, lookouts and monuments to the very famous Captain James Cook.

The beaches that fringe these shores provide some of the most crystal blue waters you will ever have the pleasure of swimming in. Though during the stinger season which is between the months of November through to May it is always suggested that you make use of the enclosed swimming areas or put on a stinger suit if you are going into the water. Though all of this aside it still isn't a deterrent for thousands of people each year who come to Cooktown to venture into the waters. You will have on your doorstep the World Heritage Great Barrier Reef so dive on in and explore the every changing and awe-inspiring coral reefs.

Outside of Cooktown you can wander through lush tropical rainforests, swim in rock pools, visit plunging waterfalls and amazing national parks. So many outstanding tour operators run daily trips throughout the region so that you can have the chance to experience the best parts all for yourself.

So make the choice today to come to tropical haven of Cooktown for a holiday that will have your forgetting about your everyday stresses of life and just let you relax and kick back!

Attractions

Cooktown has over two centuries of rich history. Cooktown was the site of the first white 'settlement' in Australia when Captain James Cook, having accidentally struck the Great Barrier Reef, off the coast north of Cape Tribulation, struggled up the coast and beached the Endeavour on the shores of the Endeavour River. Cook and his crew were to stay on the edge of the Endeavour River from 17 June to 4 August, 1770, the longest time they were to spend at any location in Australia.

Discover the most beautiful, lush natural settings of Cooktown. Naturally there are the pristine beaches, but you can also find tropical lagoons, waterfalls, hidden gardens, and magical mountain views.

A must-see is a visit to Grassy Hill Lookout where you can experience 360 degree views of the countryside and beaches. There is also a walking track from the summit to the nearby beach at Cherry Tree Bay.

Cooktown, with it's anchor and cannon recovered from the reef that wrecked Captain Cook's "Endeavour", is a fascinating place. Located in far north Queensland Australia, the fishing is great and the scenery is unique. Cooktown also has an Airport.

Cooktown Attractions and Activities

A visit to the Museum and the historic cemetery should be on everyone's list, followed by an afternoon at the Fishermans Wharf to watch the barramundi being caught and the sun set. Explore Cooktown's history and culture, not only by walking through town, but also by visiting the monuments and museums of Cooktown.

James Cook Museum

James Cook Museum is located on the corner of Helen Street and Furneaux Street. Built as a convent in 1889, Cooktown's finest historical building houses well-preserved and presented relics from Cook's time in the town, including journal entries and the cannon and anchor from the Endeavour, retrieved from the sea floor in 1971, and displays on the area's Indigenous culture. Entry is $10 for adults, children $3. Opens at 9:30, closes at 4pm.

Nature's Powerhouse

Home to two excellent galleries: the Charlie Tanner Gallery, with pickled and preserved creepy-crawlie exhibits; and the Vera Scarth-Johnson Gallery, displaying botanical illustrations of the region's native plants.

The centre doubles as Cooktown's official visitor centre, with brochures outlining some of the area's excellent walking trails. Its Verandah Cafe serves dishes, such as gado gado with coconut damper. Nature's Powerhouse is at the entry to Cooktown's 62-hectare Botanic Gardens. Filled with native and exotic tropical plants, including rare orchids, the gardens are among Australia's oldest and most magnificent.

James Cook Museum (National Trust of Queensland)

Housed in a stunning 19th century convent building, the James Cook Museum is one of Queensland's best museums, showcasing the fascinating history of Cooktown. The museum follows the story of Captain James Cook's enforced seven week stay at the Endeavour River, during which the first meaningful contact between Europeans and Indigenous Australian took place, to the days of the Palmer River gold rush, as well as personal stories and items from Cooktown's early residents.

The museum is also where Cookstown's visitor information centre is housed.

A rare, nineteenth century brick building of substance, constructed during the period of the 1880s boom, James Cook Museum shows the evolution of education in remote regions of Queensland. Five Sisters of Mercy arrived in the goldfield port of Cooktown in 1888. St Mary's Convent, designed by architect FDG Stanley, opened within a year. As well as regular classes, music, dancing and deportment were taught to boarders and day students until 1941.

Contact details
Address: Cnr Helen & Furneaux Street, Cooktown, Qld, 4895
Email: jamescookmuseum@nationaltrustqld.org
Phone: 07 4069 5386

Nature's Powerhouse

Nature's PowerHouse, a large interpretive centre stunningly situated within Cooktown's historic Botanic Gardens, houses the nationally significant Vera Scarf-Johnson botanical illustrations, a natural history display, gift store, and café, as well as being the Cook Shire Visitor Information Centre.

Email: info@cooktowns.com

David Mills

VIC phone number: 07 40696 004

Nature's PowerHouse contact details:

Email: chill@kindredcafe.com.au
NPH phone: 07 40 695 763

Cooktown Creative Arts Association

The Cooktown Creative Arts Association Shop is located in the Old Cooktown Railway Station building in Charlotte Street. Being in the main street of Cooktown, it provides local artists and crafts people with a wonderful venue to display and sell their hand made arts and crafts.

There are displays of wood work, furniture, paintings, jewellery, stained glass, quilts, cane baskets, silk paintings, T-shirts, post cards, etched glasses and photography. Customers are welcome to browse through the shop and enjoy the wide range of art and craft produced by the talented local artists.

Contact details
Address: 97 Charlotte Street, Cooktown, Qld, 4895

Phone: 07 4069 5794

Cooktown Bowls Club

With social lawn bowls on Wednesdays and Saturdays, meals available 7 nights from 06:00pm and the occasional entertainment, the Cooktown Bowls Club has something to offer for the whole family. Don't forget to book ahead!

Contact details
Address: 129 Charlotte Street, Cooktown, Qld, 4895

Email: info@cooktownbowls.com.au

Phone: 07 4069 5819

Things to See and Do

Down Charlotte Street

The best way to start appreciating the richness of Cooktown is to take a long and leisurely walk down the main street (Charlotte Street). On one side are impressive historic buildings - a reminder of the wealth that once flowed through the town - and on the other side is parkland with a variety of memorials as well as unique attractions like the Singing Ship and the unusual sculpture celebrating the contribution of the Chinese to the community.

Cook Memorials

There are no fewer than six Cook monuments in the town. There is a cairn at the place where he beached the *Endeavour*, another smaller monument a few metres away, a Bicentennial statue of the Captain in a nearby park, and a huge civic monument on Charlotte Street which was designed by George St Paul Connolly in the office of the Queensland Colonial Architect and built in 1887.

Cook Remembers the Endeavour River

Cook had successfully sailed through the Great Barrier Reef until 10 June, 1770. His diary entries for the night of Sunday 10 June and the morning of Monday 11 June 1770 record the events: "The shore between Cape Grafton and the above northern point forms a large but not very deep bay, which I named Trinity Bay, after the day on which it was discover'd; the north point Cape Tribulation because here began all our troubles.

"Before 10 o'Clock (p.m.) we had 20 and 21 fathoms and continued in that depth until a few minutes before 11, when we had 17, and before the man at the lead could heave another cast the ship struck and stuck fast."

Cook's vessel, the H.M. Barque *Endeavour,* ran onto a section of the Great Barrier Reef now known as Endeavour Reef. It managed to continue up the coast to the Endeavour River near present-day Cooktown. Cook and his crew stayed on the river's edge from 17 June to 4 August, 1770.

Cook's Journal records: "18 June 1770. I climbed one of the highest hills among those that overlooked the harbour, which afforded by no means a comfortable prospect; the lowland near the river is wholly overrun with mangroves, among which the saltwater flows every tide; and the high land appeared everywhere stony and barren. In the mean time, Mr Banks had also taken a walk up the country and met with the frames of several old Indian houses, and places where they had dressed shellfish.

Then on "30 June 1770. And went myself upon a hill which lies over the south point, to take a view of the sea. At this time it was low water and I saw, with great concern, innumerable sand banks and shoals lying all along the coast in every direction. The innermost lay about three or four miles from the shore, the outermost extended as far as I could see with my glass, and many of them did but just rise above water. There was some appearance of a passage to the northward and I had no hope of getting clear but in that direction; for as the wind blows constantly from S.E., it would be difficult, if not impossible, to return back to the southward." It was the first "settlement" of Europeans on the east coast of the continent and it makes Cooktown a hugely important historic site.

Cook Monument and Cannon

Not surprisingly the most impressive monument in town is the huge work designed by George St Paul Connolly in the office of the Queensland Colonial Architect and built in 1887. The cannon next to it was brought to Cooktown in 1885 to repulse a possible Russian invasion. So pervasive was the belief that the invasion was imminent that the Cooktown Council sent a wire to the Queensland Premier "requesting he supply arms, ammunition and a competent officer to take charge against a threat of Russian invasion." The cannon, which had been cast in Scotland in 1803, was duly sent along with 3 cannonballs, 2 rifles and an officer. It is still fired once a year during the Cooktown Discovery Festival.

Musical Ship

Located in the park beside the waterfront, the Musical Ship is fitted with marimbas, thongaphones, tok-toks, chimes and doof (bass drum) and is a very entertaining interactive sculpture. It is a unique 8.5 metre sculptural installation made from recycled poly-pipe, stainless steel, aluminium, and Ironwood with sea creature inserts designed and painted by local Aboriginal artists Helen Gordon, Conrad Michael and Joseph McIvor. It was "launched" in 2007 as part of the Queensland Music Festival, and designed and built by Steve Langton with his team at Hubbub Music. Commissioned by Queensland Music Festival's Artistic Director, Paul Grabowsky, the project was supported by Cook Shire Council.

Edmund Kennedy Memorial and Others

Next to the Cook statue in the park is a tribute to Edmund Kennedy, honouring his journey from Rockingham Bay to Escape River. The memorial was unveiled in 1948 exactly 100 years after Kennedy's death.

There's also a monument to Dan Seymour who established the National Riding Track from Melbourne to Cooktown in 1977. The trail was mapped between 1974 and the 1980s.

There's a cannon which was brought to the town to prevent an unlikely attack from the Russians. "The cannon was cast in 1803 in Carron, Scotland. During the height of the 'Russian invasion' scare of 1885, the Cooktown Municipal Council telegraphed to the Premier of Queensland, requesting him to supply arms, ammunition and an officer to take charge of the Cooktown volunteer defence force. This cannon was sent, along with 3 cannonballs, 2 rifles and 1 officer. Initially the cannon was located on the foreshore near the Powder Magazine on Webber Esplanade, overlooking the entrance to Cooktown Harbour on the Endeavour River estuary. It is fired once a year as part of the annual Cook's landing re-enactment celebrations."

Mary Watson's Monument

In 1880 Captain Robert Watson, a beche-de-mer (sea cucumber) fisherman, arrived on Lizard Island with his wife, two Chinese servants and baby daughter. He built a cottage just along from the present site of the Lizard Island resort. The ruins are still visible.

In September 1880, during one of Captain Watson's absences from the island, Guugu Yimmidir Aborigines from the mainland attacked the cottage and killed one of the Chinese servants, Ah Leung. Mrs. Watson, accompanied by her child and the other Chinese servant (Ah Sam), leapt into a water tank (it can be seen in the Townsville Museum - it is a large rectangular tub) which was used for boiling beche-de-mer. The vessel floated away from the island but they could not steer it to the coast. All three died of thirst. When their bodies were eventually found they were buried in Cooktown cemetery. On Charlotte Street is a memorial to Mary Beatrice Watson. It is a fine example of Victorian Gothic design, was funded by public subscription and erected in 1886. It was designed and built by Ernest Greenway.

River of Life Walkway

Along the footpath on the waterfront side of Charlotte Street there are a large number of tiles stretching for 500 metres. The winding pathway features hand-painted and carved ceramic tiles with a mixture of both minimal and very detailed designs. Some, like the man who saved his dog from a crocodile, are amusing. Others are stories about the town. Seven local artists, helped by Townsville potter Shelley Burt, created the artworks. Their artistic brief was to depict the diversity of Cooktown's present-day identity, contrasted against that of its cultural history.

The Westpac Building

Located at 120 Charlotte Street, the Westpac Bank, with its superb cedar joinery and heavy masonry columns, was completed in 1891. At the time it was the Queensland National Bank and was designed by FDG Stanley, who designed a number of bank buildings in the 1880s and 1890s. The premises were purchased by the Bank of New South Wales (the precursor to Westpac) in 1934 and restoration work has been undertaken since then.

The Queensland Heritage Register notes that the building is: "a two-storeyed brick building with a corrugated iron roof and timber verandahs to three sides. It has a rendered street facade, with a substantial colonnade to the ground floor, a more delicately detailed upper storey, and a central entrance portico. The building has an L-shaped plan. The street-facing wing has the bank on the ground floor, with a public banking area to the north-west, and the managers residence above, with bedrooms and lounge overlooking the street.

An adjoining wing extending to the rear contains staff quarters and a single storeyed kitchen.

The ground floor colonnade comprises round rendered concrete columns with an entablature with rectangular motifs, and a rendered concrete balustrade with shaped balusters. The first floor has cast iron columns with floriated capitals, a wrought iron balustrade, and a timber frieze. The entrance portico has paired columns to the ground floor flanking an arch with a keystone. An arched pediment spans the width of the entry, and is surmounted by a projecting bay with arched timber work and a triangular timber pediment. The eaves have shaped timber brackets, and a rendered masonry chimney rises above the roofline. Windows and doors to the ground floor street facade are arched, linked with string courses, and decorated with keystones. The upper level openings are rectangular.

Cooktown Post and Telegraph Office

Located at 121 Charlotte Street, and previously the Cooktown Shire Council and now the Cooktown History Centre, the building now offers an award winning interpretative display which allows visitors to appreciate the rich history of Cooktown and the surrounding area. The building is listed on the Queensland Heritage Register which notes that it: "was constructed in 1876-77 as Cooktown's first purpose-built Post and Telegraph Office. Its function changed to that of municipal council offices in 1893, and it has retained this function for over a century." It notes that the "post and telegraph offices were designed in the office of the colonial architect, FDG Stanley. As colonial architect, Stanley also designed the Cooktown Powder Magazine [1874] and the first wing of the Cooktown Hospital [1879], and in private practice prepared plans for St Mary's Convent at Cooktown

[1888-89] and the former Cooktown Queensland National Bank [1890-92].

The Boathouse

Located on Charlotte Street between the Post Office and the History Centre, The Boathouse is the official home of the Cooktown Re-enactment Association. It contains murals depicting the story of Captain Cook's historic forty eight days at the Endeavour River; his eight meetings with the Guugu Yimithirr Bama people; scenes sourced from the journals of Cook, Joseph Banks and Sydney Parkinson; images of Cook and a "Little Old" Guugu Yimithirr man reconciling after a dispute over Cook's refusal to share turtles; images of the H.M. Barque Endeavour stuck fast upon the Great Barrier Reef; a map of the Guuu Yimithirr lands around the Endeavour River; and other animals seen here for the first time were the crocodile, dingo, possum, flying fox, quoll and many species of animals, fish, birds, shells and insects never before seen by Europeans.

Bank of North Queensland

Located at 126 Charlotte Street, the Bank of North Queensland (sometimes known as the Ferrari Estates Building) was constructed in 1890-1891. The Queensland Heritage Register notes: "The building remains a rare example of its type: a substantial, two-storeyed late 19th century North Queensland bank building containing banking chamber and manager's residence, constructed of rendered brick, with front and side verandahs to the upper level, illustrating the adaptive use of design in a remote tropical locale."

They place it in the larger economic context of "When the Cooktown branch was established in 1888, alluvial goldmining on the Palmer River gold fields was still paying high dividends, the Annam tin fields had just been opened, and the local bêche-de-mer industry was booming. Cooktown, which serviced a district population of approximately 30,000, was thriving, and both the Bank of New South Wales and the Queensland National Bank had opened branches there already. Such was local business confidence in the future of far North Queensland, that within two years the Bank of North Queensland had commissioned Townsville architects Eyre & Munro to design substantial new premises for the Cooktown branch.

Cooktown Cemetery

The cemetery at the western end of Charlotte Street has a large map indicating the location of tombstones and other sites of interest. These include the sepulchres of William Hovell, the hapless Mrs. Watson, the mysterious Normanby woman (a white woman who was found living with

Aborigines in unexplained circumstances), the victims of at least two shipwrecks, and a special section for non-believers and Aborigines. In total there were 1,830 burials between 1877 and 1920

There is also a Chinese Shrine. Over 20,000 Chinese passed through the town on their way to the goldfields and, at one time, Cooktown had a separate Chinatown with a permanent population of nearly 3000 people. The Queensland Heritage Register records: "The cemetery bears testimony to the diverse nationalities who came to Cooktown and the Palmer goldfields in the late 19th century, and includes the graves of French, Chinese, English, Swedish, Germans and South Sea Islanders. Of particular prominence are the Chinese - mostly gardeners, miners, labourers and storekeepers - who account for approximately one-sixth (about 300) of the burials in the period 1877-1920. It is understood that most Chinese initially interred here were later exhumed and returned to China. The contribution of the Chinese to the development of Cooktown and the Palmer River goldfields in the late 19th century cannot be underestimated. As late as 1901, when the population of the Palmer River goldfield was just 600 persons, 377 of them were Chinese, and Chinese accounted for approximately 7.5% of the population of the Cook and Palmer census districts. In 1887 the local Chinese community erected a Shrine in the cemetery to honour their dead.".

The 'Off To Seek His Fortune' Statue and Landing Place

To the east of the town, on the foreshore, is a statue of an old gold prospector with a pan under one arm and a pick in his hand. The plaque reads: "At this spot on 24th October 1873, the vessel "Leichhardt" discharged its cargo of government officials, miners, horses and supplies for the trek to the Palmer River. This was the start of the famous "Palmer River Goldrush", and the birth of the port of Cooktown. Miners from all around the world, numbering in the tens of thousands, quickly followed. The flow of people, supplies and gold through the port established Cooktown as one of Queensland's most prosperous town and the state's second busiest port. ... This statue represents a typical miner on his way to the goldfields in the 1870s, and was commissioned by the Cooktown and District Historical Society to mark the 125th Anniversary of the establishment of Cooktown. 31 October, 1998."

Nearby is a sign explaining that it was near this spot on 18 June, 1770 that Cook, 86 men, livestock of sheep, pigs, dogs, ducks, hens and a goat reached the safety of the riverbank. There are quotes from the various journals for 18 June:

Cook - "At 1 p.m. the ship floated and we warped her into the harbour and moored her alongside of a steep beach on the south side."

Banks - "so near the shore that by a stage from her to it all her cargo might be got out and in again in a very short time."

Parkinson - "We set up tents ashore, unloaded her, carried all the cargo and provisions into them, and there lodged and accommodated our sick."

Chinese Migrants

At the end of Charlotte Street, near the waterfront, is an interesting sculpture of three Chinese figures. As the signage explains "Chinese migrants had an important, but underrated, role in developing Australia's north. This sculpture celebrates their contributions. The seated new arrival contemplates his new country before the trek to the goldfield. The two standing figures represent those who later prospered and contributed to Australian business, services and commerce." The sculpture is by Hans Pehl an Atherton Tablelands artist blacksmith.

Cooktown Powder Magazine

Further east along the foreshore, and designed by Francis Drummond Greville Stanley and built in 1875-1876, the Cooktown Powder Magazine is one of the earliest known surviving Government powder magazines in Queensland. The reason it was built was that under the Navigation Act of 1876, the master of any ship entering a Queensland port with gunpowder to be unloaded, had to ensure that it was placed in a government magazine. The magazine was built to deal with gunpowder that would be used at the Palmer River goldmines. The Department of Public Works called tenders for a powder magazine at Cooktown in July, 1875. The contract, which was for a brick store 26 feet by 15 feet, roofed with galvanised iron and surrounded at a distance of 25ft by a 7ft high timber fence, was won in September 1875 by HJ Meldrum, with a price of £590. For safety reasons, the structure was to be located at the rocks by the sea at the northern edge of Grassy Hill, a considerable distance from the pilot station. It is now owned by the National Trust.

James Cook Historical Museum - St Mary's Convent and School

Located on the corner of Helen and Furneaux Street, the James Cook Historical Museum was originally St Mary's Convent which was built in 1888-1889. A magnificent two-storey structure it was constructed in the belief that the town would become an important port. The elaborate cast-iron columns and balustrades reflect a sense of certainty. The Queensland Heritage Register sees the building's significance as "its rarity value: few late 19th century buildings of this substance and decorative detail were erected in centres as remote as Cooktown, accessible only by sea in the 1880s" and "The former convent and school is an excellent, highly intact example of a substantial, 1880s boom era brick institutional building with decorative detailing, designed to accommodate the tropical Cooktown climate and to cater for both convent and school purposes.

The museum recommends that each visitor spend at least an hour looking at the exhibits, which include a Chinese joss house (originally brought from Canton), a shell collection, interesting material on Cooktown's early history, and artefacts from the *Endeavour*, including one of the cannons jettisoned from the vessel when it ran aground on Endeavour Reef, and one of the ship's anchors which was also recovered from the reef. The National Trust website notes: "The Endeavour

Gallery not only explores the fight for survival Cook and his men faced on the reef, it also documents the many discoveries made by the ship's scientific team during their enforced stay at the Endeavour River.

Integral to Australian history and cultural identity is the interaction between Cook and the local Guugu Yimithiir people the most extensive he experienced in Australia and this story is told from both perspectives. Other museum galleries explore the changing face of Cooktown. The galleries on the ground floor former classrooms and the school hall house objects from pupils and Sisters who called the convent home, tales from the Palmer gold rush and a display dedicated to the rich Chinese heritage of the region. The Nuns' cells and dormitories on the upper floor are home to exhibits detailing the strong maritime history of Cooktown and the personal stories and objects from local families who, although they endured hardship, loneliness and isolation, nevertheless carved out a life in this remote and often unforgiving location. The Indigenous Gallery provides an unmissable insight into the culture and history of the Guugu Yimithiir people." The museum is open from 9.00 am - 4.00 pm each day (it is closed Monday between October and April), tel: (07) 4069 5386..

Nature's Powerhouse

Located on Walker Street opposite the Botanic Gardens, Nature's Powerhouse houses the Vera Scarth-Johnson botanical illustrations and a natural history display. It is part of the Cook Shire Visitor Information Centre and is open from 9.30 am - 4.00 pm seven days. Tel: (07) 4069 6004.

Grassy Hill and the Lighthouse

A steep winding road leads to Grassy Hill which

provides panoramic views of the coast, the Endeavour River and Cooktown. At the top of the hill is a monument to Cook as well as the lighthouse. A nearby placard reprints a section from the *Cooktown Courier* of 5 August 1885 which notes: "We understand that our lighthouse is on board the *New Guinea* which left Batavia on 27 July for Queensland ports. We have here another proof of the government's desire to deal fairly with us. Before long the bright rays of our lighthouse will be gleaming over the waste of waters, carrying comfort and an assurance of safety to mariners who have to thread the intricate navigation of our coast...no better monument could be erected to the memory of Captain Cook. It is the one he himself would have chosen, as it will recall the gallant navigator and explorer every time its bright tower of white light is seen."

The *Australian e-Heritage* portal points out that the lighthouse "was erected in 1886 at a cost of £842/8/7 for the building and £156 for the lighting apparatus - a 4th Order Fixed Dioptric Light 180 made by Chance Bros & Co., Lighthouse Works, near Birmingham. GP Heath supervised the placing of the apparatus in the completed tower in mid-September 1886. It was a manned light, lit by kerosene." .

Other Attractions in the Area

The Bloomfield Track from Cooktown to Daintree
From Cooktown to Cape Tribulation the road, which was built by the local council (ably encouraged by Premier Joh Bjelke-Petersen) in 1983 despite passionate protests from environmentalists, is challenging and, in the minds of many, a road that should never have been constructed. It is an ugly dirt-red gash across the

face of the rainforest which is characterised by unbelievable gradients, narrowness, bulldust, cavernous potholes in the dry season and quagmires of mud in the wet. It is for 4WD vehicles only.

Of course the road travels through incredibly beautiful country. If you are determined to make the journey make sure you visit the Wujal Wujal Falls (a thirty minute walk from the track); pause and inspect the Wujal Wujal Arts & Cultural Centre which is open from 10.00 am - 4.00 pm and has interesting examples of local Aboriginal art; and marvel at the strange Black Mountain, a mountain of black granite boulders which looks as though it has been placed beside the road by some giant. It is known as Kalkajaka ('place of the spear') and is an important meeting place for the Eastern Guugu-Yimithirr Bama Aborigines. Visitors are advised not to venture onto the boulder field.

The real challenges of the route are:

(a) the Bloomfield River is tidal and cannot be crossed in safety at high tide or when there has been rain. Every driver needs to determine, with care, when low tide is occurring and aim to get to the river as close to that time as possible.

(b) the road becomes impossible during the wet season because the bulldust turns to mud and there are washouts and collapses.

Bloomfield Lodge

Located south of Cooktown in the heart of the Daintree Rainforest at the mouth of the Bloomfield river is Bloomfield Lodge. It is not cheap. However the setting is glorious and if you want to experience what it is like to live in a rainforest on the edge of the Coral Sea, and eat and be treated to five star service, then Bloomfield is about as good as it gets.

Bloomfleld Lodge is located on the coast some 120 kilometres south of Cooktown and deep in the Daintree Rainforest. The only access is by water and, if you are alert, you can see the local crocodiles lazing in the mud on the banks of the Bloomfield River as the boat takes visitors from the local airstrip across the estuary to the Bloomfield jetty.

The tides are so large, and the mouth of the Bloomfield River so shallow, that the boat carrying visitors nudges towards the lodge until it runs aground some distance from the shore at which point a tractor is backed into the water and hooked onto the boat.

A short walk up the hill and you are in a rainforest paradise. There's a freshwater pool with deck chairs; a huge, open-air al fresco dining area; and on narrow bush tracks and across a swinging bridge are cabins with overhead fans, elegant mosquito nets and wooden-shuttered windows that gaze out through the canopy across the appropriately named Weary Bay.

Restricted to only 36 visitors, Bloomfield Lodge is a unique destination where the emphasis is on relaxation and rainforest experiences. It is possible to hire a boat and go out to the Great Barrier Reef for either snorkelling or big game fishing but the emphasis is on the lodge's two main, and free, activities. There is a guided rainforest walk lasting two to two-and-a-half hour which does nothing more than make its way up the narrow valley behind the lodge, reach the top of the hill and then descend down the other side. Led by a well-informed guide it includes sightings of rare orchids, exotic lichens and the possibility of seeing the magnificent Ulysses butterfly.

The Bloomfield River cruise, also lasting two to two-and-a-half hours, heads up the Bloomfield River to the causeway at the local Aboriginal community of Wujal Wujal. Most trips include sightings of saltwater crocodiles which glide through the river's muddy waters searching for places on the banks where they can laze and bask in the sun.

Black Mountains (Kalkajaka) National Park

Located 25 km to the south of Cooktown on the Mulligan Highway these strange mountains feature huge granite boulders (some the size of a suburban house) blackened by surface lichen. The geology of the mountains is explained on the National Parks website: "Around 260 million years ago, a mass of molten rock (magma) slowly solidified deep below the earth's surface, forming a body of hard granite rock. As softer land surfaces above eroded away, the sparsely fractured top of this granite was gradually exposed. Weathering and chemical decomposition removed loose material along weak fractures extending downward through the rock.

More resistant rock remained as large rectangular blocks, their corners becoming progressively rounded into boulders. The solid granite core of the mountain now lies beneath the jumbled cover of boulders. The granite rock is actually a light grey colour and composed of mineral such as feldspar, mica and hornblende. Black Mountain's distinctive dark appearance is due to a film of microscopic blue-green algae growing on the exposed surfaces. Grey patches and boulder fractures indicate ongoing rock disintegration a process accelerated dramatically when cold rain hits rock, sometimes with explosive results."

The National Park is home to a diverse range of fauna and flora. Of particular interest are the Black

Mountain skink (it is distinctive because it has a duckbill-like snout and it changes from black to green when it moves from shade to sunlight); the Black Mountain boulderfrog (a frog the size of a walnut which makes a sharp tapping noise) and the Black Mountain gecko.

The rocky outcrop is of special significance to the local Guugu Yimithirr who recount a story of a feud between two brothers for the love of a girl.

Places of interest

The Boathouse, Cooktown Re-enactment Association

The Boathouse is situated on the Main Street of Cooktown, Charlotte Street, opposite the Sovereign Resort Hotel, and is home to the Cooktown Re-enactment Association.

The Cooktown Re-enactment Committee was formed in 1959 by a group of business people in an effort to kick start the local economy. The town was on a downward slide after the Palmer River gold had petered out the Laura railway was pulled up and sold for scrap iron. It was decided to perform the Re-enactment of the Landing of Captain Cook to try to encourage visitors to the community.

"Now, 53 years on, we take pleasure in the knowledge that the innovative decision of that small group of people in 1959 has worked"

The Re-enactment script was re-written in 2008 to better represent the perspective of the Guugu Yimithirr Bama [aborigine people] whose ancestors met with Cook, Banks, Solander and Parkinson 242 years ago.

Our logo Two Cultures One People was designed to reflect the feelings of the people involved and the artwork in the centre was a work by local

Indigenous artist, Mrs Helen Gordon. Around 50 people now take part in the Re-enactment every year.

The Re-enactment is a depiction of some of the unique events that took place at the Endeavour River in 1770.

Lions Den Hotel

The Lions Den Hotel is situated on the Bloomfield Track, 4km from the sealed Mulligan Highway to Cooktown or 65km north of Cape Tribulation via the 4WD Bloomfield Track. It was built in 1875 on the banks of the Little Annan River, surrounded by 100 year old mango trees and tropical landscapes. It is a landmark hotel made of timber and iron, famous for its quirky decorations and walls adorned with visitor's signatures.

Wonderfully situated in a lush valley, the Lions Den Hotel offers powered and unpowered camping (suitable for even the largest caravans and camper trailers), unique safari style lodges nestled amongst the trees, single and double room accommodation (dongas), children's playground, natural swimming holes and beautiful grounds overlooked by mysterious Black Mountain.

Whether it's a well deserved trip away with the whole family or just to drop in for an icy cold beer, come and experience the history and see a friendly face at The Lions Den!! We also offer essentials like fuel, gas and ice.

Phone: (07) 4060 3911

Fax :(07) 4060 3958

Email:info@lionsdenhotel.com.au

Mail : Lions Den Hotel

398 Shiptons Flat Rd,

Helenvale via Cooktown 4895

Walker Bay and Quarantine Bay

Both Bays can be accessed via Quarantine Bay road 5km south of Cooktown on the Mulligan Highway. To get to Walker Bay and the mouth of the Annan River, turn right just before the golf course entrance. This is a tight track that takes you through the scrub behind the beach, all the way to the river mouth. This is a popular spot for fishing, and kite surfing (no joke!- note: all beaches are crocodile habitat on the Cape, especially at the mouth of rivers)

Archer Point

The turnoff to Archer Point is about 20km south of Cooktown on the Mulligan Highway, and is 4WD recommended. It is about 15km in. There is reef close to the shore, which can be walked to at low tide, and there is a lighthouse with good views. Call the Yuku-Baja-Muliku Land Trust for more information 07 4069 6957

Cooktown History Centre

The Cooktown History Centre, run by the Cooktown & District Historical Society, offers a unique insight into the intriguing history of the area with stories, photos, interactive displays, murals and oral histories.

It is housed in the oldest building in Charlotte Street it was erected in 1875 as Cooktown's first post and telegraph office, before it was taken over by the Shire Council offices.

This stunning exhibition brings to life the historic railway, early roads, cyclones and other disasters, early families and what happened to the local indigenous people. The display is open from 9am to 3pm, Monday to Saturday, and flexible hours from October through to March. There is a small entrance fee to enable us to continue our work

121 Charlotte Street, Cooktown, QLD, 4895
Mail: PO BOX 595, Cooktown, QLD, 4895
Telephone: (07) 4069 6640
Email: cooktownhistory@gmail.com

Places to Eat

Lions Den Hotel

The Lions Den Hotel is situated on the Bloomfield Track, 4km from the sealed Mulligan Highway to Cooktown or 65km north of Cape Tribulation via the 4WD Bloomfield Track. It was built in 1875 on the banks of the Little Annan River, surrounded by 100 year old mango trees and tropical landscapes. It is a landmark hotel made of timber and iron, famous for its quirky decorations and walls adorned with visitor's signatures.

Wonderfully situated in a lush valley, the Lions Den Hotel offers powered and unpowered camping (suitable for even the largest caravans and camper trailers), unique safari style lodges nestled amongst the trees, single and double room accommodation (dongas), children's playground, natural swimming holes and beautiful grounds overlooked by mysterious Black Mountain.

Whether it's a well deserved trip away with the whole family or just to drop in for an icy cold beer, come and experience the history and see a friendly face at The Lions Den!! We also offer essentials like fuel, gas and ice.

Phone: (07) 4060 3911

Fax :(07) 4060 3958

Email:info@lionsdenhotel.com.au

Mail : Lions Den Hotel

398 Shiptons Flat Rd,

Helenvale via Cooktown 4895

Balcony Restaurant

Enjoy an a la carte menu using local produce and mouth-watering locally caught seafood, with beautiful views of the Endeavour River and Mt Saunders.

Located on the second floor of the Sovereign Resort, the Balcony Restaurant and Cocktail Bar is open for dinner April though October, 7 days a week.

Contact details
Address: 128 Charlotte Street, Cooktown, Qld, 4895
Email: info@sovereignresort.com.au
Phone: 07 4043 0500 and dial extension 470 for reservations

Annan's Restaurant

Annan's at the The River of Gold Motel is fully licensed, offering patrons excellent dining with a comprehensive menu and wine list. The bar is originally named after the Maytown township that once serviced the Palmer Goldfields and is a great place to relax, enjoy a drink and have a chat.

Both restaurant and bar are open Monday to Saturday and bookings are encouraged to avoid disappointment.

Contact details
Address: Cnr Hope & Walker Streets, Cooktown, Qld, 4895

Email: info@riverofgoldmotel.com.au

Phone: 07 4069 5222

Free Call: 1800 005 203

Restaurant 1770

Cooktown's only licensed restaurant on the waterfront invites you to join them for breakfast lunch or dinner.

Keith and Vicki offer a range of freshly prepared meals using local produce wherever possible and specialising in seafood. Combine this with homemade desserts and seriously good coffee for a memorable night out. The restaurant is right next to the town wharf so come down and check out the menus.

Contact details
Phone: 07 4069 5440

Email: therestaurant@1770cooktown.com.au

Accommodation

Cooktown Harbour Views Luxury Apartments
Situated on the main street of Cooktown, with views of the nearby harbour, these 3 bedroom apartments are fully self-contained and furnished with a large verandah and entertainment area. They are also only a short distance from other attractions in town. The facilities include air-

conditioning, a wheelchair stair lift, and secure off-street parking.

Ph: 07 4069 6633
Email: accom@cooktownviews.com

Cooktown Alamanda Inn

Our family-friendly motel provides the ideal base for your holiday in beautiful, historic Cooktown. Located a short walk from everything, Cooktown Alamanda Inn offers great value for holiday or business visits, in a tropical garden setting with glimpses of Mount Cook and the Endeavour River.

Air Conditioned Comfort

Spacious Units for couples & families

Guesthouse

Colour TV

Swimming Pool

BBQ Facilities

Guest Kitchen

Laundry

We have a range of accommodation for business and holidays, for individuals, couples and families:-

5 studio self contained units Air Conditioning, TV, fridge, ensuite, kitchenette	5 motel rooms Air Conditioning, TV, fridge, showers	5 guest house rooms Air Conditioning, TV, fridge, hand basin (share facilities) phone/fax: 07 4069 5203

Milkwood Lodge

In quiet harmony with giant Milkwood trees, the Lodge overlooks a tranquil rainforest canopy just 2 mins from the town centre and 5 mins from the golf course.

Six comfortable and secluded pole cabins each provide split level airy accommodation with en-suite bathroom and fully equipped kitchenette.

Relax under the waterfall in the saltwater pool and enjoy a meal under the stars in our barbeque area.

Ph: +61 (0) 7 4069 5007

Fax: +61 (0) 7 4069 5834

Sovereign Resort Hotel

The Sovereign Resort Hotel is a beautiful AAA 4-star rated resort situated in the heart of Cooktown, close to all historic sights, shops, wharf and museum. We have resort style rooms, deluxe rooms and 2 bedroom apartments, all air-conditioned with queen sized beds. The Sovereign Resort Hotel boasts a beautiful free form swimming pool set amidst award winning landscaped tropical gardens. They also have a wonderful Balcony Restaurant and Cafe Bar.

Bar & Bottleshop MONDAY- SUNDAY 10am to Late	Balcony Breakfast MONDAY- SUNDAY 7 am to 10am	128 Charlotte St. Cooktown, QLD 4895 info@sovereignresort.com.au T / (+61) 07 4043 0500 F / (+61) 07 4069 5582

Cooktown Holiday Park

Cooktown Holiday Park offers award-winning gardens and beautiful surroundings, comfortable fully self-contained 1 and 2 bedroom cabins, motel style units, and roomy caravan and camping sites that can accommodate large motor homes. All our sites are powered. Our camp kitchen has been voted by our guests as the best Australia has to offer.

Ph: (07) 4069 5417 Freecall: 1800 255 162
Email: enquiries@cooktownholidaypark.com.au

Cooktown Caravan Park

Operating since 2001, Cooktown Caravan Park is the newest park in town, offering caravan, motorhome and camp sites. They provide a quiet, shady and welcoming place to stay amongst 5 acres of natural bushland at the foothills of Mt Cook. The sites are shady and are home to a variety of native wildlife. The park is situated on the main road into Cooktown, approximately 1 kilometre from the town centre.

Contact details
Address: 14-16 Hope Street, Cooktown, Qld, 4895
Email: info@cooktowncaravanpark.com

Fast Guide

Climate: Cooktown is well inside the tropics, experiences the seasonal monsoon in summer, and in general has warm and dry winters. There are a couple of weeks a year in winter when the weather can get cooler and rain is more common, usually around the beginning of July. The locals will tell you that Cooktown has a couple of weeks of winter a year.

Get in

Cairns is the main access point for Cooktown, with an international airport and good bus and train connections around Australia. Most people arrive in Cooktown by car or camper.

By car: Cooktown is just over 300km north by road, from Cairns. The drive to Cooktown from Cairns is easy. The trip takes around 3 hours, is well signposted and hard to get lost. The driving challenges begin north of here.

There is a unsealed dry-weather road that cuts through the Daintree National Park following the coast. It offers better scenery, but not usually a quicker trip. Rental cars are not usually permitted on this road.

Cooktown is just over 2000km from Brisbane.

By air: Hinterland Aviation offer a regular service from Cairns to Cooktown with flights 3 times a day Monday to Friday and a Saturday morning flight.

By bus: TransNorth Bus & Coach Service travel by both the coastal and inland routes, connecting Cairns and Cooktown three times a week. The coastal service also stops in Port Douglas and the inland service in Kuranda.

Get around: The township itself is easily traversed by foot, and there are a few interesting walks to the national park and beaches that start right at the edge of town. There is a taxi service in town, and an airport shuttle.

See: You can get a combined pass to the Natures Powerhouse and the Botanical Gardens, the Bank Museum, and the James Cook Museum.

- ✓ Discovery Festival, Every June (on the June long weekend) Cooktown celebrates Cook's landing with a re-enactment.
- ✓ James Cook Museum, documents Cook's voyages, Aboriginal and natural history, the gold rush and the legacy of the Chinese miners. The museum is housed in a former convent school that was built in 1888 and run by Irish nuns.
- ✓ Bank Museum is run by the local historical society, and is a well presented history of the town.
- ✓ Grassy Hill, Close to town, provides a view little changed from that Captain Cook could

have seen. The sunsets from Grassy Hill are reknowned.

- ✓ Remains of blacksmith shop and chinese well (Turn off Bichtumen onto Oakey Creek Rd about 20km along) at the oldest mango trees in Australia.

- ✓ The concrete steps by the side of the river in the park were built for the arrival of the Queen in 1970, she disembarked there during her short but resounding visit to Cooktown.

To Do

Scenic Rim Walk

Cemetery Walk - there is a walk that starts from behind the old train station, and goes along the mangroves to the Cemetery. There are several historic graves to see.

Botanic Gardens and large bush area, with a discover visitors centre in the middle of the park. Highlight is probably the bushwalk over to Cherry Tree Bay that forms part of the Scenic Rim Walk.

Cooktown river cruise sets off daily from the wharf up the Endeavour River. Expect to see a croc or two, large varieties of mangroves, birdlife, and maybe a snake.

Musical Playground has xylophones, pipes, sails and drums. Fun for kids and adults alike, in the park next to the river.

To Buy : The Croc Shop is the souvenir destination. It is also possible to view and purchase Aboriginal art.

Cooktown is a base for supplies, and you should have no problem finding most things at the supermarkets in town.

To Eat: Expect to pay a premium over Cairns to eat out in Cooktown. There is a take-away/bakery at the southern end of town, which probably offers the best value, but closes early evening. If you don't take care of dinner early, you could be left with very few budget alternatives.

Jackey Jackey is an historic building that used to be the general store. Now a cafe, serving coffee and cake. Lacking any sort of vibe, but serving a surprisingly good cappuccino considering this is Cooktown.

The pubs and clubs server traditional pub and club fare. Expect to pay around $20+ for mains at these places.

Many of the hotels have restaurants, and there is a pizza place as well.

To Drink: There are two clubs, and three pubs in Cooktown, all are located along the main strip, and you won't have any problem finding them. The Bowls Club and the RSL Club both have a similar feel, not much to tell them apart really. The Cooktown Hotel, known only as the Top Pub is the most visitor friendly. In days past the pubs had distinct clientele, but these days you should feel comfortable having a beer wherever you choose.

Cooktown Hotel (*The Top Pub*). Meals 7 days, and accommodation.

To Sleep:

- ✓ Cairns Australia, keeps an updated list of accommodation options in Cooktown.
- ✓ Milkwood Lodge. Six pole cabins, swimming pool on the road into Cooktown.
- ✓ Sovereign Resort Hotel. 2 bedroom apartments and studios. A central pool and small tropical garden. Fronts straight onto the main strip. Nice view across to water from the

restaurant and balcony upstairs, worth going up there for a coffee. $210 per cabin, $170 resort room.

Stay safe

If you look at a brochure for Cooktown from the 1990s it will advertise beaches and swimming as a feature of the town, but all those references have been removed from any recently produced documentation. Finch Bay and Cherry Tree Bay both have nice beaches, and you can drive to Finch Bay, and walk to Cherry Tree Bay. Crocodiles have been sighted at times on both beaches, and marine stingers are present during the season.

Crocodiles and stingers also inhabit the creeks, take care when bushwalking during the wet, if the creeks are up over the track, don't cross them.

Get out

Take Oakey Creek Rd and follow the road to the oldest mango trees in Australia, planted between

Oakey Creek and Lions Creek. Over 30 tree in a line along the road about 20km off bitumen. amazing!

To continue further north than Laura requires planning. Its possible to go into the Cape Melville National Park along tracks, with a 4wd, or return to the Peninsula Developmental Road at Lakefield, to continue north to Weipa. The road is sealed and unsealed, but should be accessible to 2wd vehicles. Its essential to check road conditions, and to accept that roads can be closed quickly be rising water at creek crossings.

At Cooktown you are still 900km from the top of Australia at Cape York.

Tour

Hidden Valley Trail Rides

For a truly unforgettable experience, explore the secret trails around Cooktown on horseback.

Whether you're young, old, experienced or a beginner, enjoy a tour designed solely to match your interests, ability and schedule.

All horses are well-behaved, experienced and trained.
T/ 07 4069 6073
Mob/ 0419 816 631
E/ shagsi@hotmail.com

Cooktown Barrier Reef Fishing Charters

Locally owned and operated, this business offers tours on the reef around Cooktown for both sightseeing and fishing purposes.

Catering to various types of fishing including light tackle and bottom fishing, enjoy a fun-filled, family-friendly tour on board the 42 foot vessel "Hurricane." This boat has full bathroom facilities and is available for both day and overnight tours as well as private functions.

Snorkeling gear, camping equipment and tinnies are available to hire.
Glass bottom boat tours and morning and evening river cruises are also offered.
Senior discounts are available.

T/ 07 40695425
M/ 0457 256 783
E/ aelliott12010@gmail.com

Cooktown Barra Charters

the Endeavour River, Cooktown Barra Charters offers safe and fun fishing tours for all ages and skill levels. All fishing gear is supplied and a shade canopy is available to shield you from the elements so that you can relax and enjoy your tour.

Alongside fishing, crocodile-spotting, bird-watching, eco tours and mud crabbing tours are also available on request.

Mob/ 0408 036 887
E/ kimkomsic@bigpond.com

Cooktown Adventure Camping and Scenic Tours

With a variety of touring options available, Cooktown Adventure and Camping Safaris offers personalised tours for small groups. Whether your interests lay in camping, fishing, hunting, bird-watching or just enjoying the scenery, this company will design a tour to suit you. Explore the area around Cooktown, go out a bit further to see Lakefield National Park or go the whole hog and wander all around the Cape- Cooktown Adventure and Camping Safaris will help you have the adventure that you want.

T/ 07 4069 5889
Mob/ 0408 036 887
E/ kimkomsic@bigpond.com

Bloomfield River Water Sports

Whether you're looking to do an animal-spotting tour, a bit of fishing, hiring a boat or just getting transported to the various islands and bays around the area, Bloomfield River Water Sports has all your boating needs covered. With flexible touring schedules, fully-equipped boats and experienced staff ready to help, enjoy discovering the breathtaking scenery, abundant wildlife and historical charm that makes the Bloomfield River such a treasure.

For more information, please call 07 4060 8252.

Bungie Helicopters

Experience a scenic tour and fishing adventure like no other. Specialising in helicopter fishing trips, Bungie Helicopters allows you to experience the beauty of Far North Queensland from a unique perspective while at the same time enjoying fishing all across the Cape. With pilots who have 40 years of combined flying experience, Bungie Helicopters provides a safe, comfortable and stylish fishing tour around the Cape. They have three helicopter bases to depart from: Mossman, Cape Tribulation and Bamaga/Punsand Bay, and their tours can be tailored to suit your interests.

T/ 07 4091 4633
E/ info@bungiehelicopters.com.au

Cooktown Glass Bottom Boat and Dinghy Hire

Offering a unique way to experience Cooktown's gorgeous local waterways and coastline, enjoy a scenic, guided tour in a glass bottom boat. Spot crocodiles, birds, coral and all manner of sea life in a relaxing and informative tour.

For the more daring, hire a dinghy and set out on your adventure.
For more information contact Mark on 0427 055 481 or 0427 777 013.
Email: cooktowndinghyhire@westnet.com.au

Gone Fishing

Providing guided fishing charters and wildlife tours around Cooktown, Gone Fishing prides itself on its expert and personalised service. With a 13 year history of professional tours and 18 years of personal local fishing experience, Gone Fishing is Cooktown's longest operating and most experience guide. Whether it's fishing with lures, fly, pole or live-bait, they've got you covered.

T/ 07 4069 5980
Mob/ 0427 695 980
Email/ info@fishingcooktown.com

Daintree Air Services

Daintree Air Services do day tours to Cooktown, Lizard island, and to the Tip of the Cape, which is the world's longest scenic flight!

THE CAPE YORK TOUR Is designed to show you the highlights of Cape York, both from the air and by 4WD. Your Scenic Flight to Bamaga from Cairns is low level, covering approx. 1100 kms of remote and spectacular reefs, rainforests and outback. We will show you parts of Cape York which are inaccessible by vehicles, such as Cape Melville, the silica sands of Cape Flattery, Bathurst Heads, Princess Charlotte Bay and the Flinders Islands Group. The 4WD section of the tour takes you to Australia's Northernmost beach Frangipani Beach- via the Lockerbie Scrub and a pocket of Northern Rainforest. From Frangipani Beach we walk approx. 1000 metres to the Tip of Cape York you finally made it! You will never look at a map of Australia the same way again! You are now standing on the northermost tip of the continent. Tours can be organised from Cooktown as well as private air charters and air tours.

Bookings 1800 246 206

Yuku Baja Muliku

The Yuku Baja Muliku people are the Traditional Custodians of Archer Point, located 20km South of Cooktown. Their vision and gift to Australia is to manage Yuku Baja Muliku sustainably, to ensure its rich biodiversity and cultural integrity remain for current and future generations.

The traditional lands cover an area of 22,500 hectares and border two world heritage areas the Wet Tropical Rainforests of Queensland and the Great Barrier Reef. The region is rich in cultural sites entwined with fringing coral reefs, beaches, rainforests, woodlands, mangroves, saltpans, and sea grass beds. The rich biodiversity of the region includes turtles, dugongs, bennetts tree kangaroos, and striped possums. It also includes some of the most pristine fringing coral reefs in the tropics.

They have a number of natural resource management projects on the go, most notably their Turtle Rescue and Rehabilitation Centre. Yuku Baja Muliku is the convergence zone between healthy and stable turtle and dugong populations of Cape York and declining populations to the south, so interest and support in their activities is welcomed, with donations accepted through their website.

At present, they are currently establishing walking tracks and camping sites so their home can be shared with all. Check out their website for more information on this and other projects.

Contact details
Address: 142 Charlotte Street, Cooktown, Qld, 4895

Email: coral.hale@archerpoint.com.au

Phone: 07 4069 6957

Great Northern Tours

Great Northern Tours offer personalised, guided 4wd safaris, with a maximum of 4 person policy. Local guide David Mead is a lifelong 'birder' and 'wet tropics' certified tour guide, and has extensive experience working and travelling in Cape York.

Tailor-made itineraries are available on request to suit your time and budget. For short stays, birdwatching tours from their Cooktown base are available, allowing you to seek out some of Cape York's rare and beautiful species, close to your accommodation arrangements.

Contact details
Email: tours@greatnortherntours.com.au

Phone: 0411 348 120

Lower Cape

Attractions

Chillagoe-Mungana Caves National Park

Situated about 3 hours west of Cairns, Chillagoe can be accessed from the northern end of the Atherton Tableland via Mareeba and Dimbulah.

Some scientists believe the landscape around Chillagoe began to form about 400 million years ago, when limestone was deposited as calcareous mud and coral reefs on the bed of a shallow sea where Chillagoe is today. Subsequent tilting, folding and erosion exposed and weathered the limestone that today towers over the surrounding plains. Fluctuating groundwater levels slowly dissolved some of the limestone, creating caverns and passages, some of which have since been decorated by calcite stalactites, stalagmites and flowstones, deposited by surface waters penetrating through the rock.

There are a number of caves which can be explored via self-guided tours, as well as ranger-guided cave tours, which run daily except Christmas Day. Tickets must be purchased in advance from Queensland Parks and Wildlife Service staff based at The Hub in the Chillagoe township.

A bus service operates from Cairns and Mareeba to Chillagoe and charter flights operate from Cairns.

Please phone (07) 4094 7111 between 8:00am and 3:30pm or drop into The Hub to obtain your cave tour tickets.

Quinkan & Regional Cultural Centre

The Quinkan & Regional Cultural Centre contains a World Class Interpretive Display. QRCC is owned and operated by the local town and region. It was established with support of the Queensland Heritage Trails Network and many north Queensland organisation, business and individuals. The Quinkan Centre showcases all aspects of Quinkan Country including, Aboriginal and non-Aboriginal heritage, and the natural environment. There is something of interest for everyone from the keen fisherman to young families!

Guided tours can only be booked fthrough the Centre, including guided tours to world famous Aboriginal rock art galleries such as Split Rock, Mushroom Rock & Giant Horse Gallery and most spectacularly THE QUINKAN GALLERIES. These tours are guided by the most experienced and the leading Indigenous guides in Cape York.

The Cultural Centre also has a select range of regional Aboriginal arts and crafts and a variety of books, maps, souvenirs, Laura Dance Festival Shirts and postcards available for sale. Please contact the Quinkan Centre for further information, tour bookings and general tourist information.

Phone 0740603457 Freecall 1300594900;
Email: inquire@quinkancc.com

Hopevale Arts & Cultural Centre

In 2009, the new Hopevale Arts and Cultural Centre was opened, along with the Nganthanun Bamawi Bayan Gallery which displays locally produced arts, crafts and artifacts as well as a workshop space for local artists.

Hopevale Arts and Cultural Centre have a large range of locally made items to suit every taste and budget. While government funding supports a portion of operational costs, the centre relies on the sales of products and bookings for dance performances to maintain sustainable business.

Over 80 members utilise the centre on a regular basis to produce the art sold in the local gallery and southern exhibitions. The seasonal tourism market supports local artists as well as the Yimbaala Dance Group.

Bookings can be made with the centre to provide a traditional lunch (locally caught bush tucker and sea food cooked in a ground oven), dance performances, billy tea, weaving demonstrations, a chance to meet the local artists, interact with community members and to purchase art directly through the centre.

Free tourist information is also provided by either staff or practising artists.

Contact details
Address: 1 Flierl Street, Hope Vale, Qld, 4895
Email: adminhopevaleartscentre@bigpond.com
Phone: 07 4060 9111

Bana Yirriji Art & Cultural Centre

The Bana Yirriji Art and Cultural Centre is located on the banks of the Bloomfield River in the Wujal Wujal Community.

The artists from Wujal Wujal represent three traditional clan groups, the Yalanji, Nyungkul and Jalunji people. Inspiration comes from surrounding lands, rainforests, waterfalls, mountains,

rivers and the sea. Many of the paintings are from cultural stories passed down to the artists from their families and Traditional Elders. It is the Centre's vision to keep and hold the culture safe and sacred and to keep the community strong in mind and spirit.

All of the Centre's artworks are handcrafted and painted in the community at the Centre by local artists.

Contact details

Email: art@wujalwujalcouncil.qld.gov.au

Phone: 07 4060 8333

Accommodation

Lizard Island

Secluded from the rest of the world, Lizard Island is stunning with its 24 powdery-white beaches and 40 luxurious suites. The most northern resort in tropical Queensland, it is located directly on Australia's Great Barrier Reef.

With numerous private beaches, five star cuisine and the ultimate spa treatment available, this resort is an experience like no other. Enjoy an unforgettable holiday in this little piece of paradise.

T/ 1300 731 551 (from within Australia)
T/ (+61) 2 9538 0751 (from outside Australia)

Laura Motel

A great new option for those not wanting to camp. The motel has a range of accommodation, from single, double, twin share, family, and wheelchair friendly rooms. Reception is opposite the motel at the General Store.

Phone: 0428648672 or (07) 40603238
email: jennytavner@yahoo.com.au

Lotusbird Lodge

Named after the Jacana (Lotusbirds) that inhabit the billabong, Lotusbird Lodge is located 480 kilometres north of Cairns, and 28 kilometres east of the Musgrave Roadhouse, on the western boundary of Lakefield National Park in central eastern Cape York.

There are 10 individual pole style cabins set amongst shady eucalypts along the inner bank of a large horseshoe shaped billabong. Each cabin has its own private verandah overlooking the billabong and is very comfortably furnished, with ensuite.

The local environment ranges from open Eucalypt woodland and gallery forests, to grassy plains, marshlands, creeks and lagoons, providing the ideal habitat for over 200 species of birds making bird watching one of the major activities of the lodge. If bird watching is not your thing, the lodge is the ideal base to explore Lakeland National Park and Princess Charlotte Bay, both of which are close by.

Lotusbird is an owner operated business with 18 years experience in the Cape York tourist industry. Please contact Sue and Gary for all bookings and enquiries on the details below.</>

Contact details
Address: Marina Plains Road, Via Musgrave, Queensland

Email: info@lotusbird.com.au

Phone: 07 4060 3400

Bloomfield Beach House

Bloomfield Beach House A little bit of luxury off the beaten track….

Relax and unwind at unique Bloomfield Beach House. This remote and charming beachfront property is perfect for the ultimate getaway or luxury stopover along the infamous 'Bloomfield Track'.

This 2 bedroom (+ sleepout), 2 bathroom property caters for up to six guests, with an open plan design and modern kitchen and bathrooms.

Take a leisurely stroll along the isolated beach or bring the tinny and enjoy some fishing and crabbing in the pristine Bloomfield River.

Ph: 0438 985137

email: info@bloomfieldbeachhouse.com.au

Bloomfield Lodge

Bloomfield Lodge Luxury Eco Lodge Far North Queensland, Australia

Unique, enchanting and beautifully remote, Bloomfield Lodge is a hidden gem. A luxury boutique hideaway set in the heart of the lush tropical Daintree Rainforest and on the shores of the Coral Sea and pristine waters of the Great Barrier Reef, offering guests an unforgettable experience of two World Heritage sites. This multi award winning rainforest Eco lodge is one of Australia's most exclusive getaways, delighting its guests with gourmet dining, friendly personalised service and a rare chance to truly relax and get away from it all.

Nestling within the Daintree Rainforest on the shores of the Coral Sea, Bloomfield's uniqueness soon surrounds you. Bloomfield Lodge With a maximum of 36 guests at any one time and a member of Small Luxury Hotels, the atmosphere is intimate and relaxed, with no pressures, no formalities and no interference from the outside world. Getting there is part of the adventure. Four levels of accommodation are arranged in beautiful timber cabins designed to blend in with the surroundings, boasting superb views of the rainforest or Weary Bay. Transfers, all meals and some of a wide range of excursions are included in the price.

Ph: Reservations (07) 4035 9166
Fax: +61 7 4035 9180
Email: bloomfield@tfaustralia.com

Bloomfield Beach Camp

Situated at the northern end of the famous Bloomfield track (currently 4wd) in the little township of Ayton on the Bloomfield River, Ayton is also just 1 hour south of Cooktown on a new sealed highway.

The only camping facilities in the area, Their beach camp is 10 acres including 5 acres of spectacular rain forest, a paradise for birds both large and small and home to a variety of local wildlife.

There are shady powered as well as unpowered sites or if you fancy a bit of indulgence, there are several cabins, safari tents and even a two bedroom fully self contained cottage.

Also on site are clean toilet and shower facilities, laundry and a large, well appointed kitchen.

The camping area adjoins the beautiful Weary Bay, and is a stones throw from the Bloomfield River. The Roaring Meg Falls, high up in the Ranges makes a great outing and a great spot for a swim.

We are pet friendly and during the dry season we open a Tapas Bar most evenings.

Fishing in both the ocean and river is great for people with or without boats.

Bloomfield Beach Camp is the ideal central location for tourists visiting:

- ✓ Historic Cooktown
- ✓ Bloomfield Falls and Roaring Meg Falls (on the CREB Track)
- ✓ Cedar Bay and Black Mountain National Parks
- ✓ Daintree and Cape Tribulation National Parks
- ✓ Great Barrier Reef Marine Park and Hope Islands.
- ✓ Bloomfield River Self-drive hire boats for fishing, croc spotting or sight-seeing (no licence required) and boat transfers from Bloomfield River to Cedar Bay or Hope Island

Email: reservations@bloomfieldbeach.com.au
Phone: (07) 40608207

Hann River Roadhouse

Just 76 km north of Laura this roadhouse with campground and mechanical workshop is a great stopping point if you want to throw in a line and catch your dinner or fix your vehicle! If the fish aren't biting the roadhouse will serve you up a meal between 7.30am and 10pm (7 days a week) as well as sell you souvenirs, maps and supplies.

EFTPOS and public phone available.
For more information, please call 07 4060 3242.
Fax: 07 4060 3399

Cape Tribulation Camping

Cape Trib Camping is nestled in the Daintree Rainforest, boarded by the golden sands of Myall Beach and the turquoise waters of the Great Barrier Reef.

Situated 2.5 hours north of Cairns on the sealed coastal road, halfway between between Cairns and

Cooktown. Explore and discover one of the world's oldest surviving rainforests with a huge range of activities and adventures on offer.

Cape Trib Camping has a range of beachfront camping and accommodation ideal for couples, familes and groups to relax, unwind and recharge.

Phone (07) 4098 0077

Fax (07) 4098 0075

Address: Lot 11 Cape Tribulation Road, Cape Tribulation, QLD 4873

Email: stay@capetribcamping.com.au

Palmer River Roadhouse

Located 80 km north of Mount Carbine on the Mulligan Highway, Palmer River Roadhouse is a good refreshment and accommodation stop on the drive from Cairns to Cooktown.

The Palmer River Roadhouse is situated on the historical Palmer River site of the original gold rush.

The Roadhouse has 22 powered caravan and camp sites and 4 permanent tented sites, as well as a free museum.

There are bar/dining and BBQ facilities, clean rest rooms and free entry to the museum. Fuel is available, and they have awesome steak sandwiches!

Ph: 07 4060 2020

Email: palmerriverroadhouse@activ8.net.au

Mount Carbine Caravan Park

MT Carbine Caravan Park is ideally located for the traveller wishing to explore Far North Queensland -whether it be the Palmer River Gold Fields, Lakeland Downs with its vast cropping areas, the Annan Gorge, the mysterious Black Mountains, the

Mt Mulligan Coal Field, the beautiful Daintree Rainforest and historic Cooktown.

While you are relaxing in our peaceful surrounds, enjoy activities that include bird watching, bushwalking and there are a multitude of 4WD tracks for the enthusiast.

MT Carbine Caravan Park is located near the following Major Centres:

135 km north-west of Cairns

68 km north of Mareeba

197 km south of Cooktown

70 km west of Port Douglas

Come and stay with us in the former Mining Village at "MTCarbine Caravan Park" and explore some of MT Carbine's unique history.

Facilities include clean amenities, gas barbeque, tennis and basketball courts. Campfires are permitted, a shop, pub and fuel facilities are nearby, and daily guided tours are available. Pets conditional.

Ph: (07) 4094 3160

Email: mt_carbine@reachnet.com.au

Places of Interest

Daintree

The only place in the world where two World Heritage-listed sites exist side by side Daintree National Park and The Great Barrier Reef!

Here you will find coastal ranges covered in some of the oldest tropical rainforest in the world, stretching all the way to the beach, and overlooking the world's most extensive coral reef system. Take the Great Barrier Reef Drive north from Cairns to Cape Tribulation, and experience the many pristine beaches and awesome views, as this route winds its way along the coast and through the forested mountainside.

There are many places to stay, and activities to suite all ages and budgets. Some of the things you may want to try are:

- ✓ Crocodile and wildlife spotting tours of the Daintree River;
- ✓ Sea Kayaking;
- ✓ Jungle Surfing;
- ✓ Horse Rides along the beach;
- ✓ Rainforest Boardwalks;
- ✓ Fishing tours;
- ✓ Tropical fruits;
- ✓ And much, much more!....

To plan your trip through this stunning region of North Queensland, go to the Destination Daintree website check out what's on offer-
Phone Number: 1800 174 895

Pormpuraaw

The Pormpuraaw Deed of Grant in Trust (DOGIT) occupies 466,198 hectares and is approximately 700 km west of Cairns, on the west coast of Cape York.

Pormpuraaw has a population of approximately 630 (as of June 2001), with about 90% of the total population being of Aboriginal or Torres Strait Islander origin.

Pormpuraaw Community lands are being increasingly exposed to tourism, especially through traffic travelling up through the Alice and Mitchell Rivers National Park from the Gulf Savannah and south, rejoining the Peninsula Development Road at Musgrave Roadhouse. Pormpuraaw Council envisages a capability to deal with the recreational fishing fraternity who may not be able to be accommodated on Kowanyama lands.

They have established two official camping areas, (both with septic and showers) one at the mouth of the Mungkan River, one at the mouth of the Chapman River at either end of the Pormpuraaw airstrip and are considering a freshwater base for visiting anglers. There is also a guesthouse within the village which is used mainly by itinerant contractors and public servants.

There is a council fuel pump, community store, kiosk and a coffee shop. There is a health clinic and the council workshop does basic mechanical repairs. Contact Parmpuraaw Community Council on 07 4060 4600.

Phone Number: 1800 174 895

Laura
Gold mining and pastoralism are the industries which have given birth to the townships of Coen

and Laura which are now significant service centers for travellers. These townships are home to a number of third generation pastoral families with historical association within the area and Aboriginal clan groups including Gugu Ballanji, Ayapathu, Gugu Minni, Lama Lama Port Stewart, Lakefield Gugu Thaypan, Northern Kaanju, Gugu Warra, Olkolo, Gugu Yimithirr, Southern Kaanju, Gugu Yulanji, Umpila, Olkolo and Wik Peoples.

With a population fewer than 100, Laura is a small town that boasts a hotel, motel, general store, two service stations, a school, police station,and a health clinic. Visitors can take in the Quinkan Cultural Centre which depicts indigenous, pioneering and contemporary life in Cape York and veiw the world's largest known Aboriginal rock art gallery. The district is home to dozens of Aboriginal art gallery sites, only a few of which are open to the public and some only after formal application to the Aboriginal Ranger at Laura.

Contact Cook Shire Council on 07 4069 5444

Kowanyama

The name Kowanyama means "The place of many waters." The community is situated on the banks of the Magnificent, a tributary of the Mitchell River 20 km inland from the coastline of the Gulf of Carpentaria. Kowanyama is accessed by an all weather airstrip, as well as unsealed roads in the dry season from Pormpurraw to the north, Normanton to the south and Cairns to the east.

Kowanyama is a Deed of Grant in Trust (DOGIT) land which comprises the direct descendants of the Indigenous habitants of the Lower Mitchell and Alice Rivers and neighbouring areas now held by pastoral tenants. These include the Kokoberra, Yir Yorant (or Kokomnjen) and Kunjen clans.

The Kowanyama community has a population of approximately 1,200 (2001), with about 93% of the total population being of Aboriginal or Torres Strait Islander origin.

There is a designated tourist season, which extends from June 1st to October 1st. Kowanyama provides four public camping areas, with two campsites apiece, and is very popular with fishing enthusiasts.

Kowanyama has a small supermarket that sells fresh foods, packaged and frozen foods, and hardware items. The store is similar to a medium sized IGA store. The store is operated by DATSIP, and the manager is able to obtain any goods that are not normally kept for sale.

The coffee shop operated by the Anglican Church, a fully air-conditioned Coffee Shop stocks take away food, entertainment media and small goods. There is a guest house in the community. The Kowanyama Canteen operates Monday to Friday, from 3:30 pm to 8:30 pm. Patrons may buy light beer only.

For access to Kowanyama lands contact the council office.
Kowanyama Aboriginal Shire Council Telephone 07 4083 7100

Hopevale

Hope Vale is situated 46 km north of Cooktown and about 10 km off the Battlecamp Road that leads to Lakefield National Park and Laura.

Hope Vale was established as a Lutheran Mission in 1949. The community covers an area of 110,000 hectares and is a Deed of Grant in Trust (DOGIT) land.

Today's population is estimated at 830 (2001), with approximately 94% of the total population being of Aboriginal or Torres Strait Islander origin from various clans including the Dhuppi, Nukgal, Binthi, Thitharr, Dharrpa, Ngayumbarr-Ngayumbarr, Dingaal, Ngurrumungu, Thaanil, Gamaay, Ngaatha, Burunga .

In addition to these clans, the community is made up of the Kuku Yimidhirr speaking peoples, the Yiidhuwarra (traditional owners of Barrow Point, Flinders Island, and the South Annan), the Bagaarrmugu, Muunthiwarra, Juunjuwaara and Muli peoples plus the Gan Gaarr and Bulgoon peoples to the south, the Kings Plain's Thukuun Warra and the Sunset Yulanji peoples in the Maytown area.

Visitors requiring access to the Elim Beach can obtain a permit ($10) from the service station or Eddie's Camp on the beach. Hope Vale has a good general store (with ATM) but is closed Sundays. Post office and banking services are available at the Council Administration Offices during regular office hours.

Contact Hope Vale Community Council Telephone 07 4060 9133

Central Cape

Roadhouses are conveniently spaced along the Peninsular Development Road, providing food and fuel, as well as accommodation; enabling you to travel all the way to the top without camping, should you wish to. There is a general store in Coen, and supermarkets in Weipa, Lockhart River, and Bamaga. The Roadhouses are a great place to stop and meet some of the locals, so you can get updates on road conditions, and possibly some 'inside information' on some of the lesser known attractions. Travelling north you will pass Lakeland Roadhouse, Laura Roadhouse, Hann River Roadhouse, Musgrave Roadhouse, Archer River Roadhouse, Moreton Telegraph Station, and Bramwell Junction at the start of the Old Telegraph Line track and Bypass Roads. You can stop for a swim along the way, in the shallow sandy rivers of Coen and Archer River.

An hour or two past Musgrave Station is Coen, a township of around 300 people, situated along the Coen River. There is free camping at the Gold Mine on the way into town, or along the river north of town; there is a drop toilet here.

About 70km north of Coen is Archer River Roadhouse, on the banks of the River. They have a big camping area with many facilities, including hot showers, toilets, washing machines, and noncamping accommodation. The roadhouse has fuel, a café, a bar, and they do some mechanical repairs.

The Bamaga Road has two bypass roads which detour the Old Telegraph Track (OTL), allowing travellers to drive to The Tip without having to negotiate the rough OTL. These pass through the highlands to the east and west of the OTL. This section has the iconic waterfalls of Fruitbat, Twin, and Eliot falls. Fruitbat Falls are just an easy 5 minute drive in, but Twin and Elliot are about 15 minutes in, and have a creek crossing which can get deep.

Places of Interest

Wunthulpu Visitor Centre, Coen

On the way into Coen is the Wunthulpu Visitors centre. Wunthulpu is a story place in the Coen area associated with the Bone Fish which is one of many Ayapathu people stories of Cape York. The Wunthulpu Visitors centre is owned and operated by Wunthulpu Aboriginal Land Trust which was established in 1997. The Current site which the centre is set on was the old Aboriginal Reserve in the Town of Coen, and the centre now displays old photos of the old reserve, early settlement and Artefacts.

The Visitors Centre has tourism merchandise, Aboriginal art and artefacts, refreshments, including Espresso Coffee, Driver Reviver cups of tea and Coffee, information and seasonal guided Pig Hunting on the trust land. The centre is open from 8.30 to 4.30 pm daily during the tourism season.

For more information, call the centre on (07) 40601282

Coen Heritage House

At the southern end of the main street is the Coen Heritage House, with displays about local history, including information on the Gold Rush, local families, and the building of the Telegraph Line.coen heritage h4

A collection of mining equipment, previously part of the Cape York Mining Museum in Weipa, is also on display.

The End

www.ingramcontent.com/pod-product-compliance
Lightning Source LLC
Chambersburg PA
CBHW031123080526
44587CB00011B/1082